W9-BKA-269

Great Britain

Helen Arnold

RSVP

RAINTREE STECK-VAUGHN
P U B L I S H E R S
The Steck-Vaughn Company

Austin, Texas

Published by Raintree Steck-Vaughn Publishers, an imprint of Steck-Vaughn Company

A ZOË BOOK

Editor: Kath Davies, Helene Resky
Design: Jan Sterling, Sterling Associates
Map: Gecko Limited
Production: Grahame Griffiths

Library of Congress Cataloging-in-Publication Data

Arnold, Helen.
    Great Britain / Helen Arnold.
       p. cm. — (Postcards from)
    "A Zoë book" — T.p. verso.
    Includes index.
    ISBN 0-8172-4005-5 (lib. binding)
    ISBN 0-8172-4226-0 (softcover)
    1. Great Britain — Juvenile literature. [1. Great Britain.]
  I. Title. II. Series.
  DA27.5.A84 1996
  941–dc20
                                               95–15828
                                                  CIP
                                                       AC

Printed and bound in the United States
1 2 3 4 5 6 7 8 9 0 WZ 99 98 97 96 95

Photographic acknowledgments

The publishers wish to acknowledge, with thanks, the following photographic sources:

DDA Photo Library / Paul Juler 28; The Hutchison Library / Stephen Seque - title page; Robert Harding Picture Library 8; Impact Photos / Simon Shepheard 12; / Alain Le Garsmeur 16; / Tony Page 26; David Williams Picture Library - cover bl, 20; Zefa - cover tl & r, 6, 10, 14, 18, 22, 24.

The publishers have made every effort to trace the copyright holders, but if they have inadvertently overlooked any, they will be pleased to make the necessary arrangement at the first opportunity.

Contents

A Map of Great Britain 4

In the Middle of London 6

A Boat Trip 8

An Old Tea Shop 10

Traveling Around 12

A Trip Across the Channel 14

On the Beach at Blackpool 16

A Castle in Wales 18

A Lake in Scotland 20

A Visit to Cambridge 22

Stonehenge 24

Canterbury Cathedral 26

The British Flag 28

Glossary 30

Index 32

All the words that appear in **bold** are explained in the Glossary on page 30.

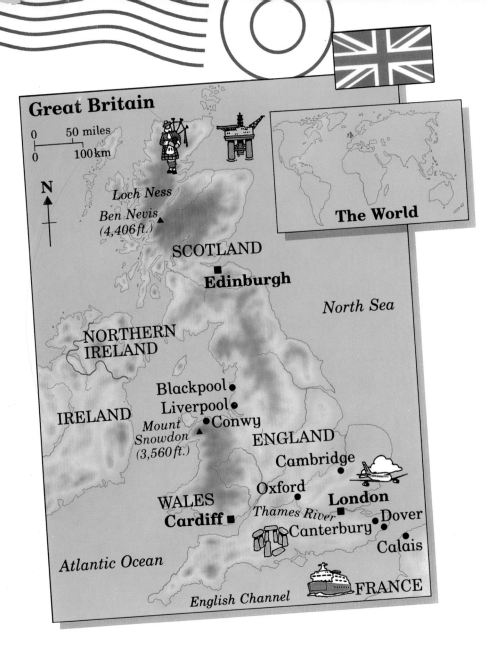

Great Britain

0   50 miles
0   100 km

N

Loch Ness
Ben Nevis
(4,406 ft.)

SCOTLAND

Edinburgh

North Sea

NORTHERN
IRELAND

Blackpool
Liverpool
IRELAND   Mount   Conwy
Snowdon
(3,560 ft.)

ENGLAND

Cambridge

Oxford

WALES   London
Cardiff   Thames River
Canterbury   Dover
Calais

Atlantic Ocean

FRANCE

English Channel

The World

A big map of Great Britain
and a small map of the world

Dear Estelle,

It took us almost 8 hours to fly to London from Chicago. England is part of Great Britain. It is marked in red on the small map. The country is small, but many people live here.

Love,

Renee

P.S. Dad says that we will visit Scotland and Wales. These countries are also part of Great Britain. People in Northern Ireland are ruled from Great Britain, too.

The Tower of London, England

Dear John,

We are staying in London. It is the **capital** city of England. This castle is about 1,000 years old. It is close to the Thames River. We went there on a **subway**.

Your friend,

Will

P.S. Mom says that long ago the tower was used as a prison. Now the tower is a **museum**. The Crown Jewels, which the kings and queens of England wear, are kept there.

The Thames Barrier, London

Dear Rosie,

Today we went on a boat to the Thames **Barrier**. We saw new tall apartments and old buildings. I liked the clock tower called Big Ben the best.

Love,

Sharon

P.S. Dad says that we could not see much of the Thames Barrier because it is under the water. It can be raised to make a wall or barrier across the Thames River. This stops the river from flooding London.

A tea shop in Lavenham, Suffolk, England

Dear Nick,

Some of the houses here are more than 400 years old. We had buns with cream and jam at this old tea shop. Mom paid with English money, which is called pounds and pence.

See you soon,

Pat

P.S. Mom says that long ago Lavenham was a rich market town. People bought and sold wool here. They used some of their money to build a big church. I guess that is why it is called a wool church!

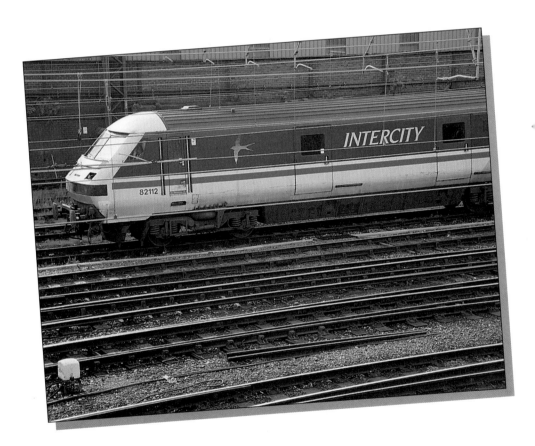

A train at Euston Station, London

Dear Juliet,

We went north to Liverpool on a train like this one. My grandmother lives there. There was a telephone on the train. Mom phoned Grandma to say that we were on the way.

Yours,

Adam

P.S. Dad says that most people here live in towns. They like to live in houses with gardens. Many people travel by train each day to work in the cities.

A hovercraft from France landing at Dover, England

Dear Phil,

Dover is only 22 miles (35 km) away from Calais in France. People go on day trips across the English Channel. We went on the **hovercraft**. It took about 40 minutes to get to France.

Your brother,

Andy

P.S. We saw the signs for the Channel Tunnel near Dover. The tunnel goes under the water to France. You can travel through the tunnel on the train.

Blackpool beach, England

Dear José,

It was too cold to swim here, but we went for a donkey ride. We played a game of **cricket** on the beach. Then we had **fish and chips**. Blackpool Tower is lit up at night.

Yours,

Lee

P.S. Mom says that some British families go to hot countries for their vacations. Even in the summer the ocean feels cold here. It rains a lot, too! That is why the fields are so green.

Conwy Castle, Wales

Dear Erica,

We went up the highest mountain in Wales yesterday. It is called Mount Snowdon. Today we went to see this castle. We could walk on the walls at the top. We heard people speaking Welsh in Conwy.

Your sister,

Mary

P.S. Dad says that the castle was built about 700 years ago by an English king. The king built many castles in Wales.

Loch Ness, Scotland

Dear Ben,

There are stories, or **legends**, about a monster that lives in this *loch*. That is the Scottish word for a lake. Tomorrow we are going to Edinburgh. It is the capital city of Scotland.

Yours,

Colin

P.S. My friend Kirsty says she comes here every summer, but she has not seen Nessie. That is the nickname for the monster. I did not see Nessie either!

The Bridge of Sighs, Cambridge, England

Dear Rochelle,

We came to Cambridge to see my sister Jo. She is a student here at the **university**. We went on a boat like this one. It is called a **punt**. Then we went to play soccer in the park. I love playing soccer!

Yours,

Mel

P.S. Mom says that most children leave school when they are 16. Some go on to study at universities such as Oxford or Cambridge.

Stonehenge, Wiltshire, England

Dear Marie,

This circle of stones is huge. It is about 3,000 years old. No one knows why the circle was built. There are stone circles in other parts of Great Britain. Stonehenge is the biggest one.

Yours,

Debra

P.S. Dad says that some people think stone circles were huge calendars. They showed the position of the sun and the stars during the year.

Canterbury Cathedral, Kent, England

Dear Barbara,

We have seen many churches and **cathedrals** in Great Britain. Canterbury is an old city near Dover. Many **tourists** come to see the city and the cathedral.

Your friend,

Shirley

P.S. Mom says that Canterbury has been the the most important cathedral in England for more than 800 years. It is the world center for **Christians** who belong to the Church of England.

The British flag flies in the
city of London.

Dear Grant,

The flag for Great Britain is called the Union Jack. The flag for England is white with a red cross. The flag for Scotland is blue with a white cross. The colors on the Union Jack come from these flags.

Yours,

Shane

P.S. I like the flag for Wales best. It has a red dragon on it. The queen does not rule Great Britain now. The people choose their leaders. Great Britain is a **democracy**.

Glossary

Barrier: Something that keeps one thing away from another. Walls and fences are barriers.

Capital: The town or city where people who rule the country meet. It is not always the biggest city in the country.

Cathedral: The most important Christian church in an area of a country. The leader of the churches in the area is called a bishop.

Christian: People who follow the teachings of Jesus. Jesus lived about 2,000 years ago.

Cricket: A ball game played by two teams in a field using two bats

Democracy: A country where the people choose the leaders they want to run the country

Fish and chips: Fried fish served with french fries

Hovercraft: A machine that travels over water or land on a cushion of air

Legend: An old story that many people believe, even though it may not be true

Museum: A building where interesting things from the past are on display

P.S.: This stands for Post Script. A postscript is the part of a card or letter that is added at the end, after the person has signed it.

Punt: A boat with a flat bottom

Subway: A train that runs under the ground

Tourist: A person who is on vacation away from home

University: A place where people go to study after high school

Index

beaches 16–17
Blackpool 16–17
boats 9, 15, 23
buildings 9, 11

Cambridge 22–23
Canterbury 26–27
castles 7, 18–19
Channel Tunnel 15
children 23
churches 11, 26, 27
cities 7, 13, 27

Dover 14, 15, 27

Edinburgh 21
England 5, 6, 7, 27, 29
English Channel 15

families 17
food 11, 17
France 14, 15

kings 7, 19

lakes 20–21
Liverpool 13
London 7, 9, 28

mountains 19

ocean 17
Oxford 23

queens 7, 29

rivers 7, 9
rulers 29

schools 23
Scotland 5, 20–21, 29
sports 17, 23
stories 21

towns 11, 13
trains 12, 13, 15

vacations 17

Wales 5, 18, 19, 29